The Art of Confidence:
A Survival Guide For Teens

By Terry Trower LMHC

This book is dedicated to the awesome teens in our world, as well as the "inner teen" in all of us.

If you're between the ages of 13 and 20, you're probably facing many challenges. The teenage years are not for sissies!

These are the years when you're an explorer…discovering who you are, and what you want to do, be, and accomplish in your life. Maybe the main accomplishment you want at this point is to have friends and graduate. These are great goals too!

So, let's explore some of the problems and the challenges you, as a teenager, may encounter. These problems can eat away at your self- confidence, leaving you feeling down on yourself and destroying any sense of your total awesomeness. Self -confidence is a strength you're going to need.

Being a teenager is a bit like living on two different planets. On one planet your goal is to differentiate yourself from everyone else…to find out what makes you, you…to discover what makes you tick, what makes you unique, and what your true beliefs are about life.

This is because your brain has recently changed from concrete thinking, where you take things very literally, to abstract thinking, where you develop your ability to analyze and form opinions on more abstract subjects.

I'll give you an example. I once asked one of my ninth- grade students how he saw himself. He told me he saw himself as being a little shy.

Yet, when I asked a 5th grader how she saw herself, she gave me a funny look and said, "in a mirror." That's when it hit me.

Transitioning from concrete thinking, which happens around the age of 11 or 12, to abstract thinking, is like going from knock - knock jokes to Latin 101…a giant leap forward.

Because your brain is operating in abstract mode, you're now equipped to tackle more abstract subjects such as "Who am I?" and "What do I want to do with my life?" On the other hand, you may be thinking, "I just want to know what's for lunch, and what to do this weekend."

This brings me to your other planet …Planet Conformity. On this planet you're willing to throw away certain facets of your individuality in order to fit in. Fitting in is like being able to breathe. It feels like oxygen and without it you'll die…or at least feel like dying.

So, how do you reconcile the two? The easiest explanation is that they're both parts of you.

You have a part that wants to be recognized for the unique individual you are. Another part though, wants to be exactly like your friends, or, at the very least, appear to be.

It's like you're on a journey but you haven't quite reached your destination, and you're not totally sure where that destination lies.

Scary? Yes, but exciting. You get to chart your own course. You're the captain of your ship.

So, let's talk about how to get around the ice-burgs…because they're there.

Questions for Discussion:

1. What are the biggest challenges for teens today?

2. What are your solutions to these problems? If you had the power, what changes would you suggest?

3. What small step can you take at this time to get the ball rolling?

Ice-burg #1-

Not Knowing Your True Self

You're either not sure who you are, or you have a false sense of who you are. And if you don't have a strong sense of who you are, you'll allow others to define you. During the teenage years, others will be happy to define you, and you might not like their definitions.

How do you end up with a false sense of who you are? How does this happen?

As you might guess, it begins when you hear messages about yourself that aren't true, that don't reflect the real you. The damage is done when you believe these messages.

Did you know that your character and personality is basically formed by the age of 7? Your brain isn't fully developed until the age of 25, but your basic personality and belief system is alive and well by the age of 7.

The truth is…during your first 7 years, you're being programmed with the beliefs of your caretakers, probably your parents. It's like being in a hypnotic trance. You have all these beliefs, but don't remember where they came from. You've basically adopted the beliefs of your parents or other important people in your life at that time. This is who you are. And this is a good thing. It gives you a sense of identity. But what if some of these beliefs about yourself are what we call limiting beliefs, like "I'm not very smart, or I'm not talented, or I'm not loveable, or I'm not good enough." Where did these come from?

Young children typically don't censor what they say because they haven't yet developed social skills. Those kids in the sandbox can say some pretty mean things. These mean words can seep deep into your psyche and then you've got a limiting belief about yourself. And these negative beliefs are like velcro. They stick!

If this sounds like you, you may feel like you're the only kid on the planet with these limiting beliefs. But, guess what, and I hope you're sitting down… everyone has these beliefs. It's like a computer program silently running in the background of your mind, affecting everything you do, say, or aim for.

One way to combat these limiting beliefs is to reprogram yourself by building a list of your strengths. Once you start running this program instead, you'll have more confidence.
And don't underestimate the power of knowing your strengths.

You may be thinking this sounds too easy and probably won't work. If so, you're correct in thinking it's not easy. Think of yourself as a pie with many pieces. Your negative beliefs are merely pieces of the pie. You can also create pieces of positive beliefs based on knowing your strengths.

The problem is… most people can rattle off a long list about what's wrong with them, but don't have a clue what's right with them. So, arm yourself by knowing your strengths.
Once you know your strengths, and the more you focus on them instead of your weaknesses, the more self -confidence you'll feel.

A great way to find out what your strengths are is to ask the people who know you best, your friends and parents. A lot of times, people don't tell you what they like about you, or what they admire about you, because they think you already know. And maybe you do know. But by asking your parents and friends, people who already like you, you'll add to your arsenal of strengths. You can even think of your strengths as your shield…your defense against mean remarks, or your own self-doubt. It's a powerful weapon.

If you feel embarrassed to ask your friends what they like about you., try this…
Ask them to make a list. Then volunteer to do the same for them. It's a rare person who turns down the opportunity to hear compliments.

Here's another issue to watch out for…You may not agree with your friends. For example, you may think to yourself, "they say I'm smart, but I don't believe it." The truth is, you don't have to believe it. All you have to do is say to yourself, "They think I'm smart." If you repeat this to yourself enough times, pretty soon, even you'll start to believe it. And even if you never believe it, at least you know how others perceive you, and that's the gift your friends have given you. Don't throw that gift away.

See how powerful words can be? Even the Bible says, "In the beginning was the word". So, try to take their words into your heart. All the words spoken to you have made you who you are today.

On the other hand, if you want to have a miserable life, hang around people who don't like you. Do whatever you can to make them like you. Believe their put downs and mean comments. Spend a lot of time wondering what's wrong with you. Believe the hateful things you read on social media. Spend lots of time online trying to make people like you. Put yourself down a lot. Feel your life isn't worth living.
Forget about your strengths and your goals for the future. Now you've got it…a miserable life.

Bottom line…loving yourself is your ticket to happiness…period.

Questions for Discussion

1. Who gives you the most compliments and tells you positive things about yourself?

2. Can you remember something they said that made you feel confident? If so, write it down and read it whenever you're feeling sad. It's an instant upper.

3. Make a list of the people who are most aware of your strengths. These are the people to ask.

4. Make a list of the qualities you like and admire about your friends and family.

Ice-burg #2

The Wounded Inner Child

You may have heard the term "inner child". Of course, we don't actually have an inner child. But we all carry the feelings of childhood inside us. In that respect, our inner child is alive and well. And your inner child has lots of feelings …strong feelings. Let's face it. We're all totally helpless when we come into this world. We count on other people to protect us.

But sometimes hurtful things happen. When kids experience a lack of protection, or other traumas, they can develop a tough protective core. Their self- esteem gets damaged. So, they sometimes try to cover it up with a tough façade. The problem is…this doesn't work.

In some cases, they want others to feel the same pain they did. As a result, they take their anger out on those around them. This is a form of bullying. On the surface, they can appear to be popular, but that's not usually the case. Sometimes kids hang around them because they don't want to be the one targeted for bullying. It's more about fear than true friendship.

Of course, there are many popular kids whose popularity stems from their kindness and compassion, or because they're fun to be around. But in the case of bullies, it's usually a power trip.

One way bullies get their power is by insulting others. They're trying to pull the other person's self-esteem down to their level. The truth is…If bullies and critics could channel their energy in a more constructive way, they could actually make good leaders. They just need to tap into their strengths, talents, and gifts, which we all have been blessed with.

Bottom line…We all have wounds from childhood. But what we do with these wounds makes us either victims or victors.

Some kids use the pain from their childhood to develop empathy and compassion for others. They know how others feel because they've been there…they've felt those difficult emotions. Even though they may struggle with self- confidence themselves, they want to help others because they understand their pain.

So, what to do if you're being targeted by a bully or critic?

One of the best tactics is to surround yourself with friends who have your back.

When you have people you can talk to, it reinforces your feeling that you're ok. But what if you have few friends, or maybe even no one you call close friends?

As a former school counselor, I helped a lot of students deal with difficult issues and get through hard times. And since your peers are an important part of your life, many problems are friendship problems.

Whether you talk to you school counselor, or another person you really trust, simply talking to someone can lift your spirits and help you brainstorm solutions.

Another tactic in making friends is to make sure you know what your strengths are…and this means knowing what people like about you. You need to know what your talents and skills are, what you love to do, and what you believe in.
Knowing this makes you strong, and can even help you avoid being targeted in the first place.

 Instead of feeling devastated, deflated, and worthless when a bully (and I'm including online bullies) try to humiliate you, tap into the part of yourself that's strong and self-protective. And yes, you do have that part. It may be buried deep inside you, but it's there.

You've heard the term, "fake it 'til you make it,". Well, this is the time to put this into practice.

Even if you have no confidence in yourself, act like you do (this is what the bully does) and speak like you do. And this doesn't mean threatening or acting like the bully. Just stand tall, keep your head up, and don't feel you have to respond to the bully. Sometimes a stupid or mean comment or question doesn't deserve a reply.

If you do decide to respond, use an "I" message. For example, "I'm not answering that'" is better than, "That's a stupid question."

If the bully is insulting you online, don't respond. Anything you write online never goes away, and you can never take it back, change it, or control who sees it. I used to tell my students, "Never write or publish anything you wouldn't want to see on the evening news."

Two assets to get you through the tough times are resilience and hope. Tough times can include the death of a relative or friend, a romantic breakup, friendship problems, bullying, or periods of anxiety and depression.

Resilience is the capacity to recover quickly from your difficulties. In other words, your ability to bounce back from adversity. Here's where hope comes in. You have to have hope, or faith, that things will get better. For this, you need a plan, a written breakdown of the steps you need to take. This can be as simple as calling one friend each day. Notice I didn't say texting one friend. There's no substitute for actual voice to voice communication.

Tapping into your spiritual beliefs can go a long way in helping you through tough times. Remind yourself that tough times never last. When you're a teenager, tough times can seem permanent. The truth is...tough times do come to an end. Think of the rainbow after the storm. So, take some positive action. Then wait it out. But don't wait it out alone. That's the key.

1. In your opinion, what makes someone a bully?

2. If you had a difficult childhood, how can you set yourself up to be a victor rather than a victim?

3. Think back to a tough time in your life. How did you stay resilient during these tough times?

4. What were your main challenges during this time and how did you deal with them?

Ice-burg #3

Shyness and The Myth of Introversion

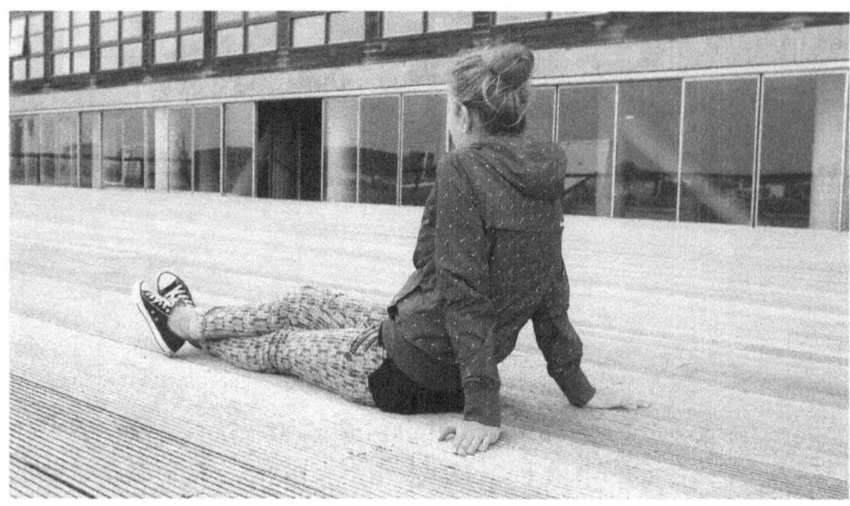

First, let's talk about shyness. If you're shy, you may be less likely to reach out to others. You might be afraid to approach people because you think you won't have anything to say.

Maybe you think being shy means you're not as worthy of attention or as cool as others. If so, don't beat yourself up because you're shy. Believe it or not, you're not alone. Over 40% of adults say they're shy.

However, shyness shouldn't stop you from having friends. Part of the problem with shyness is it makes you over-focus on yourself and how you're coming across to people. Believe it or not, most people focus on that very thing…how they're coming across. Even extroverts focus most of their attention on themselves…not on you. If you can remind yourself of this, you can take the focus off how you're coming across and place your focus on what you're wanting to say or do.

You may be thinking, "Yes, but when I try to talk to someone, I start blushing, and that's so embarrassing." Ok. Blushing is no fun. If you blush when you talk to people, don't let that stop you, though. If someone teases you, make a joke out of it. You could say, "I'm having a hot flash". Ok. That's probably a lame joke. But you can think of a joke that fits for you.

Speaking of jokes, did you know that a lot of comedians are shy? They made jokes when they were kids to cover up their shyness. And you know what? It worked. This strategy is making them a lot of money today!

If you think being an introvert means you're shy, you're wrong. Don't confuse introversion with shyness. This is the big misconception about introversion. It doesn't mean your not shy. But introversion doesn't have anything to do with shyness. Even extroverts can be shy.

 So, what is introversion and why should you care whether you're an introvert or an extrovert?

First, introversion and extroversion describe your temperament. Your temperament is not something you learn to be. You pop out of the womb as either a baby introvert or a baby extrovert, and you'll have this temperament your entire life.

It even affects your choice of friends. So, doesn't it just make sense to understand your temperament?

One of the basic differences has to do with how you re-energize. Extroverts re-energize by being around people. Introverts re-energize by having down time and being alone.

Communication-wise, extroverts rarely have an unspoken thought. They communicate often and in great detail. If you have extrovert friends, they probably like to tell you every detail of their day. It's how their brains work.

Introverts, on the other hand, have just as many thoughts, but they decide which thoughts they want to share. So, it's not unusual for people to think introverts are harder to get to know.

Friendship- wise, extroverts prefer to have a lot of friends, but their friendships are less intimate because, let's face it, they don't have time to have 25 close friends. Introverts like to have two or three close friends, but their relationships are deeper and often life -long.

This isn't to say that extroverts can't have life -long friendships. They totally can. But this is a matter of energy. Introverts like fewer friends because they can get easily drained by other people's energy. For this reason, they like smaller get-togethers rather than large parties.

And speaking of parties, if you want to meet more people, copy your extroverted friend. Notice how he or she interacts with others and try out one of their behaviors. After a while, it'll seem more natural to you.

Since temperament has a lot to do with energy, here's a good way to familiarize yourself with the effects of energy. When you've interacted with someone for a period of time, notice what's going on with your energy level.

 Do you feel energized and happy, or do you feel tired and drained? This is a way to measure which people you want to hang around, which people are energizing for you, and which people you want to avoid. Of course, there are many other qualities to consider in choosing friends, but this is a quick and easy test.

Bottom line…if you prefer to have fewer friends, it's because that's how your brain works. There's nothing wrong with you. It doesn't mean you don't have a great personality. You simply prefer fewer friends and need your down time. After you've had a little time alone, though, you're ready to roll.

Introverts…extroverts…both awesome…just different.

Questions for Discussion

1. Are you an introvert or an extrovert? Why?

2. Which situations are the most socially comfortable for you?

3. What do you guess is the #1 fear in America?

Ice-burg # 4.

Anxiety and Depression

Maybe you worry about your popularity, your appearance, your grades, or your future. This is normal. The upside of worry is when you use it to motivate you. For example, if you're afraid of failing a test, you study. You keep up with your assignments. The fear of failure makes you pro-active.

However, if you're constantly on guard and you walk around with a sense of dread, maybe it's more than ordinary worry. Maybe you're one of the millions of people who have Generalized Anxiety Disorder (GAD). So, how do you know if your worry is normal or more problematic?

According to the National Institute of Mental Health, the symptoms of generalized anxiety include restlessness, fatigue, trouble concentrating, irritability, muscle tension, difficulty controlling your worry, and trouble sleeping.

Some teens obsess over their worries to the point that they can't get the negative thoughts out of their minds. If this sounds like you, this can get in the way of everything else you're trying to accomplish, like your school work, homework, and social activities. It affects your ability to concentrate. It affects your ability to relax. It can even take the fun out of life.

One successful technique in managing worries and obsessions is to make a plan. Call it Plan -B.

 If you find yourself unable to stop a certain worry, let yourself go to the worst- case scenario because this is what your mind is trying to manage by worrying.

It doesn't work because worrying simply keeps you focused on the fear. Instead, deciding what you'll do if your worst fear comes true gives you a plan. Once you have a plan, your mind relaxes. It may not totally take away the worry, but it de-escalates it to a point you can focus on more pleasant things.

If you suffer from anxiety, there's a chance you also suffer from depression because anxiety and depression often go together. Their symptoms sometimes overlap. Depression symptoms are persistent sadness, anxiety, or empty mood, hopelessness, irritability, feelings of worthlessness, loss of interest in things you used to enjoy, fatigue, difficulty concentrating, sleep issues, changes in weight, headaches, or thoughts of death or suicide. Everyone experiences some of these symptoms. But, if you feel these symptoms every day, you may have clinical depression.

I remember, as a guidance counselor, a student telling me he felt empty. Right away, I suspected he may be depressed because a sense of emptiness indicates depression.

If you recognize yourself in these descriptions, take heart. These are treatable conditions.

You may be wondering what causes these conditions. Your anxiety or depression can be caused by problems at home, friendship issues, bullying, academic pressures, social media, health issues, your genetic makeup, or almost any situation that troubles you over a period of time.

Fortunately, there are ways to combat each of these possible causes. If you have problems at home, you need to confide in someone you trust, and this would typically be an adult.

What you need is a strategy for dealing with your problems. A parent, counselor, minister, or a trusted teacher or coach can help by listening, brainstorming, and helping you set up a plan so you can feel better.

If you choose, instead, to confide in a friend, make sure this friend is trustworthy enough to keep it confidential. If your friend tells even one other person, it's like putting an open bag of feathers in front of a fan. Just try to get those feathers back in the bag…not happening!

However, if you're having suicidal thoughts, your friend has a moral and ethical obligation to tell an adult. When a human life is at stake, this is not the time to keep a secret.

Bullying

Bullying is also a cause of depression and anxiety. Typical bullying tactics are threats, physical harm, rejection, name-calling, teasing, starting rumors, and taking personal belongings.

It may seem like a normal part of growing up, but this is no longer kid stuff. Bullying can have serious repercussions. Many adolescent suicides can be traced back to depression and despair caused by bullying at school.

And it's not just at school. Bullies also use social media, leaving you feeling like there's no escape from the harassment. Social media has made it easy to stay in touch with friends, but also made it easy for bullies to target you 24-7.

How about your own social media usage? This can contribute to your unhappiness, too.
If you're on social media for an hour, that's not a problem. But when it begins to take up giant hunks of your day, you may start to lose the ability to communicate face to face.

You could feel sad when you see others posting fun and exciting activities while you're sitting at home. It can make you feel like everyone but you is having fun! But hold on a minute…have you ever noticed that people don't post the things they don't want you to see or know? Keep that in mind the next time you're feeling jealous or left out. The truth is… they're leaving out the bad stuff.

Feeling like you don't fit in is another cause for depression or anxiety. It can make you less likely to reach out to others. Everyone feels like they don't fit in at one time or other, and this is why teens try so hard to copy other people.

The best way to find true friends is to find people who have things in common with you. This makes it so much easier to carry on a conversation because you like the same things. It also makes it easier to plan activities outside of school because you like to do some of the same things.

Finally, you can be stressed by academic pressure…pressure to pass tests, pressure to make good grades, and pressure to get into college. Here's where faith comes in to play. If you're doing your best…doing your homework, turning in assignments, studying for tests, and making decent grades, you're going to be ok. You don't have to decide what you want to do with your life in high school. And even if you do decide, that doesn't mean that's what you'll end up doing. The best formula for success is to do your best no matter where you are or what you're doing.

 A disappointment for me during my high school years was not going to the college of my choice. But I ended up absolutely loving the college that I had as a back-up, Oklahoma State University. In fact, I think the universe had my back by not giving me my first choice.

I also remember having lots of trouble declaring a major. On the first day of orientation, an advisor asked me what my major was going to be. I was so clueless, I responded by saying, "What's a major?" He explained that your major is the primary subject you study. You usually aim for a degree in that area.

Because I loved my high school journalism class and wrote for the school paper, I said, "Journalism." But that didn't last long. I soon changed my major from journalism to psychology to teaching and back to psychology about 3 times. And that was ok. How can you possibly know, when you're 18, what you want to do? It's not a life or death decision.

If you don't like what you're doing, you can try another profession. Let's face it. You're going to be working for a long time. You have choices. The best choice is to get a degree, license, or certification after you graduate high school. In this way, you're preparing yourself to do something productive. Bottom line… do your best, stay open to new possibilities, and you'll land on your feet. I learned that you don't have to know what you want to do for the rest of your life when you're 18. Don't sweat it. You have options.

So, now that you know some of the causes of depression and anxiety, let's talk about what to do when you're feeling anxious or depressed. Some of these may sound like common sense. They're things we should all do, but often don't, either because we're too busy with other commitments or we don't consider it a priority. Yet, sometimes the simplest things are the most effective.

Often, when you're depressed, you tend to isolate. You stop calling your friends. You don't have the energy to socialize. This only deepens your depression. Although you don't feel like it, this is actually the time to reach out to friends, even if you have to force yourself to do it.

Being alone with your negative thoughts increases the likelihood you'll start to believe your negative thoughts. Now, that's a fast trip down a negative wormhole. When you're depressed, you can't really trust your thoughts. So, reach out, if only to one person.

Getting your thoughts on paper can help, too. Dr. James Pennebaker, Chair of Psychology, at the University of Texas, Austin.[1] did a research study that showed expressive writing eased feelings of depression.
His subjects wrote stories about their disturbing emotions and what happened to trigger these emotions. They were encouraged to go into great detail and not leave anything out.

If you'd like to try this technique, start by thinking about your negative emotions, as well as the negative events in your day. Then, write about it for 20 minutes for four days in a row. Don't let anyone see what you've written and don't censor what you write. To have total privacy, you might even want to shred it.

There's something powerful that occurs when you write about your feelings. It's almost like giving your feelings to the paper. I experience it as very healing and I encourage you to try it.

Mindfulness

Want a quick and easy practice to lower your stress? Mindfulness can help you feel calmer, happier, and even boost your immune system. It's not just for kids who are depressed or stressed either. It's for everyone.

What is Mindfulness, anyway? It's simply paying attention to one thing at a time. You see, multi-tasking is not all it's cracked up to be. The truth is…the more you try to multi-task by doing several tasks at the same time, the less efficient you are at each task and the more frazzled you become. It actually increases your stress! Mindfulness counteracts this.

A good way to practice mindfulness is to take 5 minutes and sit with your eyes closed in a quiet place. Just focus on your breath. When other thoughts pop into your mind, which they will, just gently go back to your breath. It's that simple. Try it. You may be surprised how many thoughts interrupt you.

The important thing is to catch yourself when you're thinking about something else and go back to focusing on the breath. This actually trains your brain to pull away from negative thoughts when they appear.

Another great exercise is just that…exercise! There are lots of articles on the positive effects of exercise on mood. Walking, running, lifting weights…these are all great ways to lift your spirits.
Often, after a stressful day at work, I stop at the gym to lift weights. I always feel calmer afterwards. If you don't like the idea of going to a gym, just walking around the block helps!

Finally, one strategy that always helps is counseling. A counselor is an impartial listener. Your counselor's only goal is to help you feel better. It's a win-win.

Bottom line…you don't have to suffer from depression and anxiety. You have a right to happiness. Even the Constitution says as much!

1. In your opinion, what causes most depression in teens? Why?

2. Why do you think the suicide rate is so high?

3. In your opinion, what needs to happen to address this problem?

4. What can you personally do to address it?

Ice-burg #5

Dating and Relationships

Building romantic relationships becomes a major goal for most teens as you move from childhood to puberty. You begin to discover feelings beyond the scope of mere friendship. How you view these relationships comes largely from how your parents treat each other, as well as how you view your personal relationship with each parent.

As a child, you observed whether relationships are loving and supportive, or abusive and full of conflict. Your parents are your first and most important relationship role models.

For better or for worse, you're often attracted to people who remind you, if only on a subconscious level, of your parents. When you're around your boyfriend or girlfriend, you carry unconscious feelings that you superimpose on that person based on the conclusions you've drawn about intimate relationships.

This, in turn, influences your behavior...how you treat them and even how you treat yourself in terms of your relationship with them. So, bottom line... you first learned about love and relationships from your family.

If your family was nurturing and supportive, as a rule, you'll have fewer relationship conflicts because you learned relationship skills from your parents. If the opposite was true, and you grew up in a home where there was lots of tension and fighting, you're probably lacking some of the basic relationship skills you need to be truly happy.

You may lack communication skills or conflict resolution skills. You may be down on the idea of marriage because you never witnessed a loving relationship.

The truth is, there are arguments and disagreements in every relationship. What's different in those that last is… people have relationships skills. And you're not born with these. You have to learn them. Learning these skills makes you relationship savvy. So, whether relationships cause you more pleasure than pain is basically up to you and your level of relationship savvy.

Did you know that your confidence level affects your love life? If your self -confidence is high, your relationship will probably run smoother. If it's low, you can expect more issues because you'll probably be looking to your partner to boost your confidence. This never works. So, that's another reason to know your strengths. Anything you do to boost your self -confidence also improves your love life.

The Signs of Abuse

Without relationship skills, you're in danger of falling into an abusive pattern without realizing it. Some teens believe abusive behavior is normal. This is because they don't understand which behaviors are actually abusive.

If this sounds like you, remember this…love isn't supposed to hurt. If people truly love you, they go out of their way NOT to hurt you. They treat you like their best friend, with kindness and respect.

Everyone has arguments and disagreements now and then, but if your relationship has more turmoil than happiness, take this as a red flag. You might be in a relationship that's going nowhere fast.

You need to be able to recognize the signs you might be in an abusive relationship. So, what are these signs?

- The most obvious sign of abuse is physical abuse. This includes hitting, slapping, pushing, and anything that feels like a violation of your personal space or makes you feel uncomfortable.
- Being threatened is another sign. This can even include threatening to break up with you if you don't do what he or she wants you to do.
- Criticism …this includes criticizing your appearance, your habits, your home, your beliefs, or anything that makes you feel demoralized or humiliated.
- Put downs…hurting your feelings. This can include saying, "I was just kidding." (If it was truly funny, you'd be laughing).
- Controlling your social life by telling you who to hang out with.
- Getting angry, upset, or jealous when you do things with your friends or family.
- Wanting to know where you are every minute of the day as well as who you're with.
- Not taking "No" for an answer…not caring how you feel.
- Pressuring you to do things you don't want to do, sexual or otherwise.
- Trying to change you.

If these behaviors are happening in your relationship, you might be in an abusive relationship. If this is the case, you'll need to get counseling or get out of the relationship. It doesn't get better.

Your attempts to win his or her approval will only make things worse and reinforce the bad behavior. A better tactic would be to learn what a normal healthy relationship looks like and start utilizing these skills with your next boyfriend or girlfriend. Remember, love doesn't hurt. Abuse, however, hurts a lot.

Dating abuse is another form of bullying. Bullies are so afraid of abandonment they'll do anything to keep you from leaving the relationship, and their techniques are usually bullying and control. But being in an abusive relationship takes a toll on your self - confidence. It makes you doubt yourself. You may know the relationship is painful, but you lack the strength to leave it.

This is where counseling can empower you to take the next step. You need to recognize when the relationship isn't good for you, no matter how much they say they love you. Remember…love doesn't hurt.

But what if you're the bully? How can you break your abusive pattern?

First, if you find yourself playing the role of the abuser in your relationship, this isn't about love. Don't fool yourself. It's about fear. It's about control. However, remind yourself that no one is perfect, including you, and you're as deserving of love as anyone.

 If you can get in touch with your strengths, and know that you deserve love as much as the next person, you won't feel like you have to control someone to keep them in your life.

Maybe you've had relationships with important people who didn't seem to love you, or treat you like you deserved to be treated. If this is true, then you know what it's like to be hurt and humiliated. The problem is you may not feel like anyone could love the real you.

But, if you can risk believing that someone can care for you with all your imperfections, which we all have, you won't have to trap or control anyone. In fact, you'll be more tolerant of the imperfections of others. You won't have to put someone down just so you can feel bigger.

When you give up control, you'll find out who really _wants_ to be with you. You won't feel threatened if they have other friends. You'll feel more secure in the relationship.

So, if you want to be happy, start by creating healthy relationships. Problem is…you probably don't have any idea what a healthy relationship looks like.

What Is A Healthy Relationship?

Let's define some of the elements of a healthy relationship.

Good communication is the life blood of a relationship. Many good relationships go awry when you mean one thing, but say another. How many times have you unintentionally alienated or angered someone by something you've said? Things can go downhill quickly with a few ill -chosen words.

How many times have you walked away from someone wondering if you've possibly offended the person? Of course, the quickest remedy for this is to check it out by asking. This puts your mind at ease, or at least gives you the chance to explain yourself.

How many times has someone told you you're too sensitive when you're hurt by something they've said? The truth is...everyone is sensitive at their core. Criticism and harsh words spoken in anger can take a long time to repair. Most people have the memory of an elephant when it comes to remembering words that hurt.

So, try this instead. If you need to address a negative situation, start with something positive. Then, take responsibility for your feelings by using the word "I" before stating how you feel.

An example would be, "I wish we could talk before school starts. I miss you when we have to wait until lunch." This goes over much better than, "Why do you always ignore me every morning?"

When you start out with a statement about what you want, the person is much more likely to listen and really hear your words.

If you start out by blaming, your friend will likely put up a psychological shield and go into a defensive mode, or simply tune you out. As you can guess, neither of these is the outcome you're looking for.

So, when you're looking for change, tread lightly. Others may look tough, but inside, we're all sensitive. Remember this rule and think before you speak. And remember, this is not a lesson learned quickly. Be patient with yourself. It takes practice.

Finally, your words are your power source. Your words either inspire or deflate.

So, start with yourself. I challenge you to find the words that inspire you, whether through poetry, song, or your own journals.

I'm personally inspired by books and poetry. My favorite poems are "**The Road Not Taken**" by Robert Frost, "**Intimations of Immortality**" by William Wordsworth, and "**Mother To Son**" by Langston Hughes.

Each of these inspire me in different ways. Each speaks to conditions we all encounter during our earthly sojourn.

If poetry isn't your thing, identify your favorite books and figure out why they move you.

 If you're more auditory, make a playlist of the songs that uplift you, and listen to them. If you find yourself longing for a place to express your feelings, start a journal.

 It's all about both knowing, and then expressing your feelings in whichever mode you choose. It will enhance your life in so many ways! Again…I challenge you…just try it!

Questions for Discussion

1. What can be done to prevent teen dating abuse?

2. What is your main takeaway from this section?

3. What qualities do you look for in a relationship?

4. What behaviors will you absolutely **not** stand for in a relationship?

Ice-burg # 6

Poor Boundaries

Another requirement for a successful relationship or friendship is good boundaries. Every pre schooler understands the concept of boundaries. Just try taking a toy away. You'll hear a loud, "That's mine!" Because even at that tender age, kids understand the idea of yours versus mine.

This is what it boils down to …what's yours is yours and what's mine is mine. If you don't want conflict in your relationship, don't take what's not yours.

This applies to material things, territorial things, your physical body, your feelings, opinions, beliefs, and values. Generally, if you feel disrespected, a boundary has been crossed.

Examples of boundaries are all around you. Drive around your neighborhood. Notice how many houses or apartments have fences. This is a boundary. Even the door to your bedroom is a boundary. If you're a teen, you might not want your little sister or brother barging in.

Touching someone inappropriately in a way that makes them uncomfortable is another boundary violation. This includes being physically aggressive, and can even be as simple as standing too close to someone.

If you cross someone's boundary without an invitation, they're going to feel violated. They'll be angry or irritated, even if they don't tell you. In fact, anger is a signal that your boundaries have been crossed.

Other examples of boundary violations are being late and making someone wait for you, cutting in front of someone in line, grabbing something away from someone, taking things off someone's desk without permission, and not returning what you borrow.

If you get your driver's license, having good boundaries becomes a safety issue. If you follow another car too closely, you're in their space, and that's a boundary violation that could cause an accident. This is just one example of how important boundaries are when you're behind the wheel!

If you're aware that someone has crossed your boundaries, the best approach is to tell the person you're not happy. You might phrase it something like this, "When you were 20 minutes late to the restaurant and didn't call me, it felt like you think your time is more important than mine. Please at least call if you're going to be late."

Now, you've defined your boundary. This is actually a test of the friendship because if the friend continues this same behavior, this person doesn't really care about your feelings, and probably isn't as good a friend as you'd hoped. Actually, this person may not be a friend at all because friends care about friends.

Honoring someone's boundaries is a measure of respect. Honoring boundaries creates trust in your relationship. People will feel safe around you. They'll trust you not to hurt or take advantage of them in any way.

Safety and trust are critical components of any good relationship. Without them, you'll never get off the launch pad!

1. Think of a time when your boundary was crossed? How did you feel?

2. Which boundary violations bug you the most?

3. Which boundary violations would cause you to end a friendship?

Conclusion

Finally, the teenage years are your gateway to the future.

You're testing new beliefs, new behaviors, and new ways of relating. You now have a human computer on top of your head with the ability to analyze data and make your own decisions.

You have a better understanding that actions have consequences. You're getting a glimpse of your next big transition...adulthood.

As you test out new roles and new behaviors, you're finding out who you want to be, as well as who you are.

Every day that your feet hit the floor, you're expanding your understanding of that glorious being called you.

When you can't understand why your friends act in a certain way, remind yourself that your own behavior is often a mystery, even to you. Life is a puzzle. You're just trying re-arrange the pieces to fit.

Hopefully, you've gained a deeper understanding of the problems and promises of being a teen. It's a wonderful time of life.

It's your first opportunity to write the script of your personal book of life, which you can edit at any time. You have the power.

To get the most from this book, review the "**Questions for Discussion**" with your friends and classmates. But, at the very least, I challenge you to answer the questions for yourself.

It's part of your ever- changing evolution. It's important to know what you think!

Bottom line…enjoy your teenage years…they won't last forever!

Bibiography

Murray, Bridget, **Writing To Heal**, American Psychological Association. June 2002, Vol. 33, No. 6

Nansel TR, Overpeck M, Pilla RS, Ruan WJ, Simons-Morton B, Scheidt P. **Bullying Behaviors Among US Youth: Prevalence and Association With Psychosocial Adjustment**. *JAMA.* 2001;285(16):2094–2100. doi:10.1001/jama.285.16.2094

About The Author

Terry Trower is a Licensed Mental Health Counselor in Florida. In her private practice she specializes in Stress Management and Life Purpose Coaching.

Terry is a former Social Studies Teacher and Guidance Counselor. She has authored several counseling publications for children and adults. These include *"The Self Control Patrol"* game and workbook and the *"Meaningful Meditation"* series.